GALLBLA

DIET COOKBOOK

FOR DIABETES

Discover Delicious, Nourishing
Recipes for Gallbladder Health and
Diabetes Management with Blood
Sugar-Balancing strategies

Dr. Kathryn F. Anderson

Disclaimer: The information contained in this book is intended to provide helpful and informative material. It is not intended to be a substitute for professional advice or guidance. Any reliance you place on the information in this book is strictly at your own risk. The author and publisher disclaim any liability or responsibility for any loss or damage that may arise as a result of the use of the information in this book.

Table of Content

Introduction

Maintaining a healthy and pleasurable lifestyle can be difficult for many people who are dealing with diabetes and gallbladder problems. The Gallbladder Diet Cookbook for Diabetes is a recipe book created to fuel your body, promote gallbladder health, and help you manage your diabetes. This cookbook, which has been painstakingly created to balance blood sugar levels and encourage a healthy lifestyle, is a veritable treasure trove of delectable recipes for breakfast, lunch, dinner, snacks, and dessert. This cookbook is your go-to source for wholesome and filling meals, whether you're looking for tasty ways to improve the function of your gallbladder or trying to keep your blood sugar stable.

Allow me to tell you the inspirational tale of Smith, a strong man whose health path took an unexpected turn when diabetes and gallbladder issues came together. Before the Gallbladder Diet Cookbook for Diabetes entered his life, Smith was faced with the difficult task of managing the dietary limitations for both diseases.

Although middle-aged professional Smith had always been aware of his health, the simultaneous advent of diabetes and gallbladder problems put him in unfamiliar ground. It was hard enough to manage dietary limitations for one ailment, but two felt like an impossible challenge. Smith found this cookbook—a gastronomic treasure that will eventually serve as his compass on the road to well-being—during one of his routine medical sessions.

Smith was drawn into the cookbook's pages by the range of recipes and the careful way in which it addressed the subtleties of blood sugar control and gallbladder health. Every meal was a thoughtfully crafted blend of tastes, textures, and nutrients to maximize his general health as well as satisfy his dietary requirements.

There were difficulties along the way. Smith experienced times of frustration and temptation, but the cookbook gave him a road plan to get over these obstacles. Equipped with delectable meals that balanced his blood sugar, Smith started to see significant improvements in his overall health.

The cookbook evolved into more than just a recipe book; it became a confidante, an empowering tool, and a force for good.

Smith's success story demonstrates the effectiveness of mindful eating, and the Gallbladder Diet Cookbook for Diabetes is an invaluable tool for anyone looking for a balanced approach to managing their diabetes and gallbladder health. Explore a gastronomic journey that will delight your taste buds and improve your general well-being by using this cookbook as a guide. It shows that a tasty, well-balanced meal can serve as the basis for a busy, healthy lifestyle.

1. The gallbladder's anatomy and operations

The gallbladder is a little, pear-shaped organ that sits below the liver and is very important to the digestive system. Even though its roles are sometimes disregarded, they are crucial to the body's overall health and the digestive process. This book examines the gallbladder's structure and functioning, highlighting the organ's significance in preserving the equilibrium of the digestive system.

Organ Structure of the Gallbladder:

- **Location:** The gallbladder is located on the right side of the belly, tucked under the liver. It is linked to the small intestine and liver by a system of ducts.

- **Structure**: The gallbladder is segmented into the fundus, body, and neck, despite its modest size. The organ helps store and release bile since it is made of smooth muscle and has a mucous membrane lining it.

- **Blood Supply**: A branch of the main hepatic artery called the cystic artery provides the gallbladder with its blood supply. This organ's circulatory network makes sure it gets the nutrition and oxygen it needs to function at its best.

The gallbladder's functions include:

- **Bile Storage**: The gallbladder's main job is to hold onto bile, which is the digesting fluid that the liver produces. The small intestine needs bile in order to break down lipids.

- **Bile Concentration**: Because the liver produces bile continuously, the gallbladder serves as a reservoir to concentrate and store this digestive juice. Concentrated bile is released into the small intestine by the gallbladder as it contracts and is required for digestion.

- **Function in Digestion**: The breakdown and absorption of fats depend heavily on bile. Fats are emulsified, or broken down into smaller pieces so that enzymes may more easily digest them. The small intestine's ability to absorb fat-soluble vitamins (A, D, E, and K) is improved by this procedure.

- **Control of Bile Flow**: Hormonal signals, in particular cholecystokinin (CCK), which is released in reaction to the presence of fats in the small intestine, control the gallbladder. The gallbladder contracts in response to CCK, releasing bile into the digestive system.

Common Disorders of the Gallbladder:

1. Gallstones: Gallstone development is a common problem involving the gallbladder. Pain, inflammation, and digestive issues may result from these solid particles blocking the bile ducts.

2. Inflammation (Cholecystitis): Cholecystitis is an inflammation of the gallbladder that is frequently brought on by gallstones. This illness, which can be acute or chronic, causes discomfort, fever, and upset stomach.

The importance of the gallbladder in the digestive process becomes clear when one is aware of its architecture and activities. The function of the gallbladder in preserving digestive balance ranges from storing bile to aiding in the breakdown of fat. A healthy diet and lifestyle are key components of proactive health management, and awareness of prevalent gallbladder problems is essential.

2. Frequently occurring gallbladder problems in diabetics

The gallbladder is only one of the many health issues that people with diabetes frequently deal with. There is a complicated association between diabetes and gallbladder problems, as diabetes affects the likelihood and severity of specific gallbladder disorders. The numerous gallbladder problems that people with diabetes may experience are examined in this book, illuminating the complex interactions between these two medical conditions.

• **Medication with Gallstones**: Gallstone development is among the most common problems. Compared to the general population, those who have diabetes are more likely to acquire gallstones. Gallstones have the potential to develop as a result of both altered bile composition and raised blood sugar levels. These tiny, hardened deposits have the ability to clog the gallbladder ducts, causing discomfort, inflammation, and even more difficulties.

- **Cholecystitis and Diabetes**: Inflammation of the gallbladder, or cholecystitis, is another prevalent issue in people with diabetes. Cholecystitis is frequently brought on by gallstones, and individuals who have diabetes may experience a more severe and apparent inflammatory reaction. Diabetes may make the inflammation worse, causing the upper abdomen to experience pain, soreness, and discomfort more frequently and intensely.

- **Delayed Gallbladder Emptying**: Due to diabetic nerve damage, the gallbladder's contraction and relaxation are not as well controlled, which might result in gastroparesis. Diabetes patients may experience delayed gallbladder emptying due to gastroparesis. The occurrence of gallstones and the possibility of problems like cholecystitis can be attributed to this slow emptying.

- **Enhanced Complication Risk:** Diabetes may make it more difficult to control gallbladder problems. Patients with diabetes may find it difficult to control their blood sugar during gallbladder-related procedures or inflammation. Diabetes can also impede the healing process, which raises the possibility of problems after gallbladder-related surgeries.

• **Obesity's Impact:** Obesity and diabetes are frequently linked. Diabetes may increase an individual's chance of obesity, which is a known risk factor for gallbladder problems. The likelihood of gallstones and associated difficulties may be increased when these factors are combined. Because diabetes and gallbladder problems interact, it's critical that people with both disorders receive comprehensive health care. A healthy diet, controlling weight, and preserving ideal blood sugar levels are all essential components of preventative care. People who manage diabetes in addition to gallbladder problems can benefit from routine monitoring and early medical intervention for any symptoms associated with gallbladder problems. This can help reduce complications and improve overall health. As usual, the key to successfully managing these health issues is seeking the counsel and treatment of medical professionals for individualized guidance.

Chapter 1: Understanding Gallbladder Health and Diabetes Management

3. How diabetes and gallbladder problems are related

The medical profession is becoming increasingly interested in the complex link between gallbladder problems and diabetes. Both disorders alone provide serious health risks, and when they come together, there may be a complicated interaction that affects the severity, risk, and course of treatment of each. We examine the relationship between diabetes and gallbladder problems in this investigation, illuminating the elements that unite these two medical conditions.

- **Same Risk Factors:** There is a connection between diabetes and gallbladder problems due to the same risk factors. Both problems are exacerbated by obesity, a sedentary lifestyle, and poor eating habits. In order to reduce the chance of having diabetes and gallbladder issues, it is crucial to address these lifestyle variables, as highlighted by the shared risk profile.

- **Insulin Resistance and Gallbladder Function:** Gallbladder dysfunction may be influenced by insulin resistance, a type 2 diabetes hallmark. Insulin regulates glucose levels and has an impact on lipid metabolism. Gallstone development may be facilitated by changes in bile composition in insulin-resistant patients due to modifications in lipid metabolism.

- **Effect of High Blood Sugar:** Diabetes is characterized by high blood sugar, which can have an adverse effect on gallbladder health. Chronically high blood sugar levels can alter the gallbladder's contractility, which can impair the organ's capacity to effectively release bile. Gallstone formation and delayed gallbladder emptying are two problems that may be exacerbated by this malfunction.

- **Hormone Release and Gallbladder Contraction:** Hormones like cholecystokinin (CCK) are released as part of the complex communication between the gallbladder and the gastrointestinal tract. Diabetes can interfere with these hormones' regular release and function, which can impact the contraction of the gallbladder. Delays in emptying and a heightened vulnerability to gallbladder troubles could be caused by this disturbance.

•   **Inflammation and Complications**: Chronic inflammation linked to diabetes may affect the gallbladder. Diabetes is also linked to a pro-inflammatory condition. An increased risk of complications like cholecystitis might result from inflammation that worsens gallbladder problems. Controlling inflammation becomes essential when discussing the relationship between diabetes and the health of the gallbladder.

•   **Management Difficulties:** Diabetes may make it more difficult to treat gallbladder problems, and vice versa. Controlling blood sugar becomes crucial while dealing with gallbladder-related issues, such as inflammation or surgery. On the other hand, in order to get the best possible healing and recovery, treating gallbladder issues in diabetics may necessitate a sophisticated strategy.

Knowing the link between diabetes and gallbladder problems helps to clarify the complex relationship between these two medical disorders. Mitigating the risks and complications associated with coexisting diabetes and gallbladder issues requires addressing shared risk factors, controlling blood sugar levels, and embracing a holistic approach to health. A thorough and individualized approach to treatment is still crucial for people managing both disorders as the study into the complexities of this connection continues.

4. Specialized diets are important for people with diabetes and gallbladder issues.

A careful and specific approach to food decisions is required when diabetes and gallbladder issues coexist, as this poses a special set of obstacles. For the purpose of controlling symptoms, enhancing digestion, and fostering general well-being, a diet specially designed to meet the unique requirements of those with both illnesses is essential. The significance of a customized diet for people coping with the intricate relationship between gallbladder and diabetes is examined in this book.

1. Blood Sugar Regulation: Blood sugar control is given priority in a particular diet for those with diabetes and gallbladder issues. Stressing high-fiber foods, complex carbs, and sensible serving sizes helps control blood sugar levels, which lessen the burden on the pancreas and lessens the effect on gallbladder health.

2. Stress on Healthful Fats: While meeting the dietary requirements of diabetics, healthy fats are essential for maintaining gallbladder health. The stimulation of gallbladder function can be achieved without sacrificing blood sugar control by choosing sources of monounsaturated and polyunsaturated fats, like avocados, almonds, and olive oil.

3. Equilibrium Macronutrients: In order to manage diabetes and gallbladder issues, it is critical to have a balance of macronutrients, proteins, fats, and carbohydrates. This equilibrium helps sustain stable blood sugar levels, boosts energy levels, and facilitates the absorption of vital nutrients.

4. Low-Glycemic Index Foods: Because low-GI foods have a milder effect on blood sugar levels, including them in the diet is advantageous for people with diabetes. Concurrently, choosing low-glycemic foods might help avoid sharp increases in insulin levels, which could affect the function of the gallbladder.

5. Moderation in the Intake of Fat: Although healthy fats are vital, moderation in the intake of fat is essential. Overindulgence in high-fat foods can lead to gallstone development, which is problematic for those who have gallbladder problems and diabetes. A customized diet finds a balance between including good fats and consuming less trans and saturated fats.

6. Foods High in Fiber and Adequate Hydration: Two essential elements of a customized diet are foods high in fiber and adequate hydration. Staying hydrated aids in digestion and reduces the risk of gallstone development. In addition to encouraging regularity and preserving healthy bowel function, fiber also enhances general well-being.

7. Tailored Dietary Strategies: A customized diet for diabetes and gallbladder issues is common since it acknowledges that each person may have different nutritional requirements. It is ensured that dietary regimens are customized to individual health profiles by consulting with healthcare professionals, including registered dietitians, and taking into account parameters like age, weight, and specific health goals.

An excellent way to manage both diabetes and gallbladder issues is with a customized diet designed for the needs of the individual. A wide variety of foods can be enjoyed while navigating the complexities of these health challenges by prioritizing blood sugar management, selecting healthy fats, balancing macronutrients, and adopting personalized nutrition plans. As with all dietary adjustments related to health, seeking advice from medical specialists guarantees that dietary decisions support general well-being and are in line with personal health objectives.

5. Fundamentals of a diabetic diet that is beneficial to the gallbladder

It takes a deliberate and specialized strategy to balance gallbladder health with a diabetic diet. For those who have both diseases, blood sugar control, and gallbladder function promotion work best together. This book provides advice on dietary choices that promote general well-being and lays out the fundamentals of a diabetic diet that is favorable to the gallbladder.

- **Give Fiber-Rich Foods Priority**

Consume plenty of foods high in fiber, such as whole grains, legumes, fruits, and vegetables. In addition to encouraging regular digestion and blood sugar regulation, fiber also increases feelings of fullness, all of which can help with weight management.

- **Select Sources of Lean Protein**

Choose lean protein sources such as beans, fish, chicken, and low-fat dairy. Saturated and trans fats, which can cause gallstones, are less prevalent in these protein choices.

- **Reduce Your Fat Intake**

Limit the amount of fat you eat overall, especially saturated and trans fats. Whereas trans fats are frequently found in processed foods and baked goods, saturated fats are found in animal products like red meat and full-fat dairy. Reducing the amount of fat consumed can help avoid gallstones and lower the chance of gallbladder inflammation.

- **Moderate Intake of Carbohydrates**

Complex carbs are preferable to refined carbohydrates for people with diabetes and gallbladder issues, even if they are still a necessary component of a balanced diet. While refined carbs, like those found in white bread, spaghetti, and sugary drinks, can raise blood sugar and contribute to the production of gallstones, complex carbohydrates, like those found in whole grains, legumes, and starchy vegetables, provide sustained energy and fiber.

- **Keep an eye on your sweetener intake**

While the occasional indulgence is acceptable, it's important to watch how much sweetness you consume, particularly if you have diabetes. Limit artificial sweeteners, which may have negative impacts on gut health, and use natural sweeteners like stevia or monk fruit in moderation.

- **Maintain Hydration**

Drinking enough water is important for good health in general and can also help avoid gallbladder issues. Make it a point to sip on lots of water throughout the day to help with digestion and stay hydrated.

- **Speak with a Certified Dietitian**

For assistance in creating a customized diabetic food plan that is gallbladder-friendly, speak with a certified dietitian or other healthcare professional. They are able to evaluate your particular requirements, make customized recommendations, and provide continuous assistance.

Extra Success Advice:

• Carefully read food labels to determine the amount of fat and cholesterol.
• Arrange your meals in advance to steer clear of impulse buys and pick healthier selections.
• Slow down, enjoy every meal, and pay attention to your body's signals of hunger and fullness when you eat mindfully.
• Exercise on a regular basis to enhance general well-being and support a nutritious diet.

Keep in mind that changing to a diabetic diet that is gallbladder-friendly takes time. Make tiny adjustments at first, and then progressively add more healthful options to your everyday routine. It is possible to attain a healthy, balanced diet that promotes the health of your gallbladder and diabetes by following individualized recommendations and making constant effort.

Chapter 2: Overcoming Nutritional Obstacles

6. Typical dietary difficulties for people with diabetes and gallbladder problems

The combination of diabetes and gallbladder problems presents special difficulties for those who are managing both ailments. It might be challenging to follow a diet that takes into account the demands of the gallbladder and blood sugar levels. This book emphasizes the delicate balance needed to support general health by examining the common dietary obstacles faced by people with diabetes and gallbladder problems.

The Health of the Gallbladder and Fat Intake

Saturated and trans fats in particular are a key cause of gallbladder issues. People who have problems with their gallbladder should consume less fat overall and opt for healthy fats like monounsaturated and polyunsaturated fats. However, because dietary fats slow down the absorption of carbs, cutting back on fat intake can also have an effect on blood sugar regulation.

Making Carbohydrate Decisions and Managing Blood Sugar

Choosing the right carbohydrates is important for diabetics since it affects blood sugar levels directly. Because of their high fiber content, complex carbohydrates like whole grains, legumes, and starchy vegetables are generally advised; but, in order to keep blood sugar steady, they must still be ingested in moderation.

Sweetener Intake and Diabetes Control

Sweeteners—natural and artificial—can be problematic for people with diabetes. Even though natural sweeteners like monk fruit or stevia are thought to be healthier than sugar, they can nevertheless have an effect on blood sugar levels. Conversely, artificial sweeteners might negatively impact intestinal health, which could make gallbladder problems worse.

Timing and Planning of Meals

Meal timing and planning are crucial for the health of the gallbladder and diabetes. While avoiding large meals or fatty foods, especially in the evening, can help minimize gallbladder discomfort, eating at regular times helps control blood sugar levels.

Handling Cues of Hunger and Fullness

Those who have gallbladder problems in addition to diabetes may find it challenging to control their hunger and fullness signals. This may result in overindulging or rash eating decisions, which may make the two problems worse. Achieving a healthy balance requires paying attention to one's body's cues and engaging in mindful eating.

Overcoming Obstacles in Diet

Those who have diabetes and gallbladder problems can use the following dietary techniques to get past these obstacles:

• **Seek Professional Advice**: To create a customized food plan that takes into account both diseases, speak with a registered dietitian or other healthcare specialist.

• **Carefully Read Food Labels**: Keep a close eye on the nutritional facts, particularly the amount of fat and carbohydrates.

• **Maintain a Carb and Fat Balance**: To keep your gallbladder healthy and your blood sugar under control, make wise decisions about the sources of your fat and carbohydrates.

- **Engage in Mindful Eating**: Take your time, enjoy every bite, and pay attention to your body's signals of hunger and fullness.

- **Schedule Meals**: To control blood sugar levels and lessen discomfort in the gallbladder, schedule meals in advance and follow regular mealtimes.

- **Incorporate Healthy Fats**: To promote general health, include healthier fats in moderation, such as those found in avocados, nuts, and seeds.

- **Pick Complex carbs**: For their fiber content and long-lasting energy, complex carbs are preferred. Examples of these include whole grains, lentils, and starchy vegetables.

- **Watch Sweetener Consumption**: Talk to your healthcare physician about artificial sweeteners and choose natural sweeteners sparingly.

Handling the nutritional difficulties brought on by gallbladder problems and diabetes needs a customized strategy and continuing assistance. Individuals can effectively manage both illnesses and achieve total well-being by forming good lifestyle habits, making educated dietary choices, and collaborating closely with healthcare specialists.

7. Ways to get over dietary limitations

It can be difficult to live with dietary restrictions, but it is possible to maintain a balanced and fulfilling diet with the appropriate tactics. Whether it's because of lifestyle decisions, allergies, or intolerances, here are some practical tips to help you get over dietary constraints and adopt a more pleasurable, healthier eating pattern.

Recognize and Comprehend Your Limitations

Start by being fully aware of the particular dietary limitations you must adhere to. Knowing your limitations—be they dietary restrictions, sensitivities, allergies, or ethical or religious considerations—is essential to making well-informed food choices.

Examine Diverse Culinary Experiences

Don't stick to your go-to dishes. Discover new recipes and ingredients that work with your limitations. Discover a world of savory and fulfilling possibilities with a little imagination and resourcefulness.

Make Advance Plans and Preparations

Following your dietary limitations might be made simpler by prepping meals and planning meals in advance. This removes the urge to reach for harmful or unattainable options during times of hunger.

Adopt Substitute Techniques

Find out about acceptable alternatives to components that are banned. For example, vegetable broth can be used as a tasty base for soups and stews, and almond flour can be used in place of wheat flour in gluten-free baking.

Make Your Needs Clearly Known

Make sure the hosts, caterers, or restaurants know about any dietary limitations you may have when dining out or at social gatherings. This guarantees that you're eating experiences will be both fun and safe.

Participate in online communities or support groups

Make connections with people who have comparable dietary constraints. Social media communities, support groups, and online forums can all offer insightful information, encouragement, and recipe ideas.

Play around with textures and flavors

Try experimenting with flavors, spices, and textures without fear. This can keep your meals exciting and varied while adhering to your dietary requirements.

Recall that overcoming dietary limitations is a process rather than a final goal. Praise your accomplishments, be patient with yourself, and ask for help when you need it. Despite any obstacles, you may continue to eat a healthy and satisfying diet by being proactive and maintaining a good outlook.

Chapter 3: Diabetic management and gallbladder health through meal planning and dish development.

8. Meal planning is crucial

Diabetes and gallbladder problems provide special dietary challenges that call for thoughtful preparation and wise meal selections. A vital strategy for controlling these illnesses, enhancing general well-being, and averting difficulties is meal planning.

- **Keeping Blood Sugar Levels Stable**

By guaranteeing a steady consumption of carbohydrates throughout the day, a well-organized meal plan assists people with diabetes in controlling their blood sugar levels. This stops blood sugar from rising and falling too quickly, which can cause a number of health issues.

- **Avoiding Discomfiture in the Gallbladder**

By avoiding large meals, particularly in the evening, and reducing total fat intake, meal planning helps reduce the risk of gallbladder discomfort and inflammation. In addition to lowering the risk of gallstones and cholecystitis, this permits the gallbladder to operate efficiently.

- **Enhancing Intestinal Well-Being**

Constipation can be avoided and digestive regularity can be enhanced by incorporating foods high in fiber into a meal plan, such as fruits, vegetables, and whole grains. Because constipation can exacerbate gallbladder discomfort, this is especially crucial for people who have gallbladder problems.

- **Improving Nutrition in General**

Meal planning ensures that people with gallbladder problems and diabetes make educated meal choices and get enough of the nutrients they need. Protein, vitamins, minerals, and healthy fats are among the essential nutrients for general health and well-being that are included in this.

- **People Manage Their Weight**

Weight control is crucial for the health of the gallbladder and diabetes, and it can be facilitated with a balanced eating plan. Gaining too much weight can exacerbate diabetes control and raise the risk of gallstones.

One cannot stress how crucial meal planning is for people with diabetes and gallbladder problems. It is an effective tool for negotiating the intricacies of both disorders, giving people the ability to make decisions that are in line with their health and well-being. With thoughtful preparation, people can take charge of their diet, effectively treating symptoms and promoting a long-term health-promoting lifestyle.

Breakfast recipes

1. Oatmeal with Berries and Nuts

Total Time: 5 minutes

Nutritional Values:

· Calories: 250
· Fat: 5g
· Carbohydrates: 40g
· Fiber: 5g
· Protein: 10g
· Sugar: 5g

Ingredients:
• 1/2 cup steel-cut or rolled oats; • 1 cup dairy- or plant-based-based milk
• 1/4 cup of mixed berries, including raspberries, blueberries, and strawberries
• 1 tablespoon chopped nuts (pecans, walnuts, and almonds)
• To taste cinnamon

Guidelines:
1. Prepare the oats per the directions on the package.
2. Spoon cooked oats into a pair of dishes.
3. Add cinnamon, nuts, and berries to the top of each bowl.

2. Whole-wheat toast with Avocado and Low-Fat Cheese

Total Time: 5 minutes

Nutritional Values:

· Calories: 350
· Fat: 15g
· Carbohydrates: 30g
· Fiber: 5g
· Protein: 15g
· Sugar: 2g

Ingredients:

½ mashed avocado

2 pieces of whole-wheat bread

• One low-fat cheese slice

• Toppings of salt and pepper

Guidelines:

Toast bread made with whole wheat.

2. Top bread with mashed avocado.

3. Add low-fat cheese on top.

4. Add pepper and salt for seasoning.

3. Scrambled Eggs with Whole-Wheat Toast and Tomato

Total Time: 10 minutes

Nutritional Values:

· Calories: 350
· Fat: 10g
· Carbohydrates: 30g
· Fiber: 3g
· Protein: 25g
· Sugar: 1g

Ingredients:

• One tablespoon olive oil; two eggs; and salt and pepper to taste
• One slice of tomato; two slices of whole-wheat toast

Guidelines:

1. Beat the eggs with a fork.
2. In a skillet over medium heat, preheat the olive oil.
3. Add eggs to skillet and cook until cooked through, scrambling frequently.
4. Add pepper and salt for seasoning.
5. Melt whole-grain bread.
6. Top toast with scrambled eggs and a tomato.

4. Fruits, veggies, and protein powder combined in a smoothie

Total Time: 5 minutes

Nutritional Values:

· Calories: 300

· Fat: 5g

· Carbohydrates: 40g

· Fiber: 5g

· Protein: 20g

· Sugar: 10g

Ingredients:

• 1/4 cup frozen berries (strawberries, raspberries, and blueberries)

• 1/4 cup leafy greens (kale, spinach); • ½ cup avocado

• A single scoop of protein powder

• One cup of milk (vegan or dairy) • Taste-tested honey or maple syrup

Guidelines:

1. Blend together all the ingredients until they are smooth.

2. Taste and add honey or maple syrup as needed.

5. Whole-wheat pancakes with Fruit Topping

Total Time: 15 minutes

Nutritional Values:

· Calories: 300
· Fat: 5g
· Carbohydrates: 40g
· Fiber: 5g
· Protein: 10g
· Sugar: 10g

Ingredients:

• One cup of whole-wheat pancake mixture
• One egg; one cup of milk, either plant-based or dairy
• Tbsp olive oil
• Your preferred fruit topping (strawberries, bananas, or sliced peaches)
• Taste-tested maple syrup or honey (optional)

Guidelines:

1. Combine the pancake mix, milk, egg, and olive oil in a big basin and whisk until well blended.
2. Turn up the heat to medium on a skillet or griddle.
3. For every pancake, transfer ¼ cup of batter onto the griddle or skillet.
4. Cook until golden brown, 2 to 3 minutes per side.
5. Add fruit topping and, if you like, maple syrup or honey over top.

6. Breakfast Burrito with Whole-Wheat Tortilla, Eggs, and Beans

Total Time: 10 minutes
Nutritional Values:
· Calories: 400
· Fat: 10g
· Carbohydrates: 50g
· Fiber: 5g
· Protein: 20g
· Sugar: 2g
Ingredients:
• ½ cup cooked black beans; 2 scrambled eggs; 1 whole-wheat tortilla
• One-third cup salsa
• Taste-tested cheese (optional)
Guidelines:
1. Use a skillet or microwave to reheat a whole-wheat tortilla.
2. Top tortilla with scrambled eggs.
3. If preferred, add cheese, salsa, and black beans on top.
4. Tightly roll up the tortilla.

7. Whole-wheat waffles with Fruit and Yogurt

Total Time: 15 minutes

Nutritional Values:

· Calories: 350

· Fat: 5g

· Carbohydrates: 45g

· Fiber: 5g

· Protein: 15g

· Sugar: 10g

Ingredients:

• Cup of whole-wheat waffle mixture

• One egg; one cup of milk, either plant-based or dairy

• Tbsp olive oil

• Your preferred fruit topping (bananas, sliced peaches, or berries) • Tasty yogurt

Guidelines:

1. Turn on the waffle iron.

2. Combine the waffle mix, milk, egg, and olive oil in a big basin and whisk until well blended.

3. Transfer a half-cup of batter onto the waffle maker.

4. Prepare waffles in accordance with waffle iron directions.

5. Add yogurt and fruit topping on top.

8. Breakfast Salad with Eggs, Greens, and Avocado

Total Time: 10 minutes

Nutritional Values:

· Calories: 350
· Fat: 15g
· Carbohydrates: 20g
· Fiber: 5g
· Protein: 20g
· Sugar: 2g

Ingredients:

• Quarts of mixed greens
• One sliced hard-boiled egg; • One sliced avocado
• Half a cup of cherry tomatoes
• One tablespoon of dressing (vinaigrette)
• Add pepper and salt to taste.

Guidelines:

1. Combine mixed greens, cherry tomatoes, avocado slices, and sliced egg in a big bowl.
2. Add a drizzle of vinaigrette dressing and adjust the seasoning with salt and pepper.

9. Greek Yogurt Parfait

Total Time: 5 minutes

Nutritional Values:

· Calories: 300
· Fat: 5g
· Carbohydrates: 35g
· Fiber: 5g
· Protein: 25g
· Sugar: 15g

Ingredients:

• A single cup of Greek yogurt
• ½ cup of granola; ¼ cup of mixed berries
• One tablespoon (optional) of maple syrup or honey

Guidelines:

1. Fill a glass or dish with yogurt, berries, granola, and honey or maple syrup (if preferred).

10. Scrambled Eggs with Whole-Wheat English Muffins

Total Time: 15 minutes

Nutritional Values:

· Calories: 450

· Fat: 10g

· Carbohydrates: 40g

· Fiber: 5g

· Protein: 25g

· Sugar: 5g

Ingredients:

• 2 eggs; 1 tablespoon olive oil; toss with salt & pepper

Toast two whole-wheat English muffins.

Guidelines:

1. Beat eggs in a bowl.

2. Place a skillet over medium heat with olive oil.

3. Put the eggs in the skillet and cook them completely, mixing them regularly.

4. Add salt and pepper for seasoning.

Serve toasted English muffins with scrambled eggs on top.

11. Whole-wheat pancakes with Yogurt Sauce

Total Time: 20 minutes

Nutritional Values:

· Calories: 400
· Fat: 5g
· Carbohydrates: 50g
· Fiber: 5g
· Protein: 15g
· Sugar: 10g

Ingredients:

• One cup of whole-wheat pancake mixture
• One egg; one cup of milk, either plant-based or dairy
• Tbsp olive oil
• Yogurt sauce: • One cup of Greek plain yogurt
• 1/4 cup chopped nuts (almonds, walnuts, pecans); ¼ cup honey or maple syrup (optional)
¼ teaspoon vanilla essence; ¼ tablespoon chia seeds

Guidelines:

1. Combine the pancake mix, milk, egg, and olive oil in a big basin and whisk until well blended.
2. Turn up the heat to medium on a skillet or griddle.

3. For every pancake, transfer ¼ cup of batter onto the griddle or skillet.
4. Cook until golden brown, 2 to 3 minutes per side.
5. In a bowl, whisk together the ingredients for the yogurt sauce while the pancakes are cooking.
6. Present pancakes with yogurt dressing.

12. Oatmeal with Cinnamon and Maple Syrup

Total Time: 5 minutes (plus overnight soaking)

Nutritional Values:

· Calories: 300
· Fat: 5g
· Carbohydrates: 40g
· Fiber: 10g
· Protein: 10g
· Sugar: 5g

Ingredients:

• 1/2 cup of rolled oats; • 1 cup of milk (vegan or dairy).

• ¼ cup chopped nuts, such as pecans, walnuts, and almonds

• A taste of cinnamon

• Maple syrup for flavoring

Guidelines:

1. Combine the oats, milk, cinnamon, and chopped nuts in a bowl.

2. Refrigerate the bowl overnight with a cover on it.

3. Taste and add maple syrup in the morning.

13. Pancakes with Chocolate Chips and Banana Slices

Total Time: 20 minutes

Nutritional Values:

· Calories: 450
· Fat: 5g
· Carbohydrates: 55g
· Fiber: 5g
· Protein: 15g
· Sugar: 15g

Ingredients:

• One cup of whole-wheat pancake mixture
• One egg; one cup of milk, either plant-based or dairy
• A tsp of olive oil and chocolate chips
• Slices of banana

Guidelines:

1. Combine the pancake mix, milk, egg, and olive oil in a big basin and whisk until well blended.
2. Turn up the heat to medium on a skillet or griddle.
3. For every pancake, transfer ¼ cup of batter onto the griddle or skillet.
4. Cook until golden brown, 2 to 3 minutes per side.
5. Add banana slices and chocolate chips while the pancakes are cooking.
6. Present pancakes topped with banana slices and chocolate chips.

14. Scrambled Eggs with Avocado and Salsa

Total Time: 10 minutes

Nutritional Values:

· Calories: 400
· Fat: 10g
· Carbohydrates: 40g
· Fiber: 5g
· Protein: 20g
· Sugar: 5g

Ingredients:

• One tablespoon olive oil; two eggs; and salt and pepper to taste
• One mashed avocado
• Any salad you like

Guidelines:

1. Beat the eggs with a fork.
2. In a skillet over medium heat, preheat the olive oil.
3. Add eggs to skillet and heat, stirring frequently, until eggs are fully cooked.
4. Add pepper and salt for seasoning.
5. Stir in salsa and mashed avocado.
6. Present salsa and mashed avocado beside scrambled eggs.

15. Waffles with Strawberries and Whipped Cream

Total Time: 20 minutes

Nutritional Values:
· Calories: 450
· Fat: 5g
· Carbohydrates: 55g
· Fiber: 5g
· Protein: 15g
· Sugar: 10g

Ingredients:
• Cup of whole-wheat waffle mixture
• One egg; one cup of milk, either plant-based or dairy
• One tablespoon of olive oil • Whipped cream • Strawberries

Guidelines:
1. Turn on the waffle iron.
2. Combine the waffle mix, milk, egg, and olive oil in a big basin and whisk until well blended.
3. Transfer a half-cup of batter onto the waffle maker.
4. Prepare waffles in accordance with waffle iron directions.
5. Add whipped cream and strawberries on top.
6. Top waffles with whipped cream and strawberries.

Lunch recipes

1. Grilled Chicken Salad with Mixed Greens, Avocado, and Vinaigrette

Total Time: 20 minutes
Nutritional Values:
· Calories: 350
· Fat: 15g
· Carbohydrates: 15g
· Fiber: 5g
· Protein: 30g
· Sugar: 2g

Ingredients:
• 2 cups mixed greens; 4 ounces grilled chicken breast, sliced
• One avocado, cut into quarters
• Half a cup of cherry tomatoes
• Two teaspoons of dressing (vinaigrette)
• Add pepper and salt to taste.

Guidelines:
1. Cook the chicken breast well on the grill.
2. Put mixed greens, cherry tomatoes, avocado slices, sliced chicken, and vinaigrette dressing in a big bowl.
3. Toss to cover.
4. Season to taste with salt and pepper.

2. Tuna Salad Sandwich on Whole-Wheat Bread with Cucumber and Tomato

Total Time: 10 minutes

Nutritional Values:

· Calories: 300
· Fat: 10g
· Carbohydrates: 30g
· Fiber: 5g
· Protein: 20g
· Sugar: 2g

Ingredients:

• Three ounces of drained canned tuna
• ¼ cup chopped celery; two tablespoons mayonnaise, either light or regular
• Two slices of whole-wheat bread; one tablespoon of minced onion; salt and pepper to taste; cucumber slices; tomato slices

Guidelines:

1. Place the tuna, celery, onion, light or mayonnaise, salt, and pepper in a bowl.
2. Top each slice of whole-wheat bread with a spoonful of tuna salad.
3. Arrange tomato and cucumber slices on top.

3. Chicken and Vegetable Skewers with Greek Yogurt Dip

Total Time: 30 minutes (including grilling time)

Nutritional Values:

· Calories: 300
· Fat: 5g
· Carbohydrates: 20g
· Fiber: 5g
· Protein: 25g
· Sugar: 2g

Ingredients:

• Four ounces of cubed, skinless, boneless chicken breast
• One bell pepper, sliced into pieces
• One onion, sliced into pieces
• One cup of plain Greek yogurt for the Greek yogurt dip
• 1/2 cup finely sliced cucumber; 1 tablespoon finely chopped fresh dill; and to taste, salt and pepper

Guidelines:

1. Set the grill pan or grill to medium heat.

2. Thread bell pepper, onion, and chicken onto skewers.

3. Cook the chicken on the skewers for ten to fifteen minutes, or until it's done.

4. Put the Greek yogurt, cucumber, dill, salt, and pepper in a bowl.

5. Present skewers beside a Greek yogurt dip.

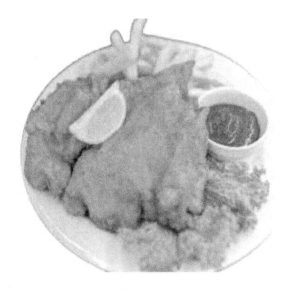

4. Lentil Soup with Whole-Wheat Bread

Total Time: 1 hour

Nutritional Values:

· Calories: 400
· Fat: 5g
· Carbohydrates: 55g
· Fiber: 10g
· Protein: 20g
· Sugar: 5g

Ingredients:

• One cup of washed dried lentils
• a single sliced onion and two cups of veggie broth
• 2 cloves minced garlic; 1 chopped carrot
1 chopped celery stalk; 1 teaspoon dried thyme; salt and pepper to taste
2 slices whole-wheat bread

Guidelines:

Lentils, vegetable broth, onion, carrot, celery, garlic, thyme, salt, and pepper should all be combined in a big saucepan.

2. Bring to a boil, then lower the heat and simmer until the lentils are soft about 30 minutes.

3. Pair whole-wheat bread with soup.

5. Salmon Salad with Mixed Greens, Avocado, and Citrus Dressing

Total Time: 20 minutes

Nutritional Values:

· Calories: 400

· Fat: 15g

· Carbohydrates: 15g

· Fiber: 5g

· Protein: 35g

· Sugar: 5g

Ingredients:

Four ounces of flaked cooked salmon and two cups of mixed greens

• One avocado, cut into quarters

• Half a cup of cherry tomatoes

¼ cup olive oil, 2 tablespoons lemon juice, 1 tablespoon orange juice, 1 teaspoon honey, and salt and pepper to taste comprise the citrus dressing.

Guidelines:

1. Put cherry tomatoes, avocado slices, flaked salmon, and mixed greens in a bowl.

2. Combine olive oil, lemon juice, orange juice, honey, salt, and pepper in another bowl.

3. Toss to coat after drizzling salad with dressing.

6. Egg Salad Sandwich on Whole-Wheat Bread with Sprouts and Cucumber

Total Time: 10 minutes

Nutritional Values:

· Calories: 350
· Fat: 10g
· Carbohydrates: 35g
· Fiber: 5g
· Protein: 25g
· Sugar: 2g

Ingredients:

• Two hard-boiled eggs, mashed; two tablespoons light or mayonnaise; and one-quarter cup chopped celery

• 2 slices of whole-wheat bread; 1 teaspoon Dijon mustard; salt and pepper to taste; Alfalfa sprouts; and cucumber slices

Guidelines:

1. Put the mashed eggs, celery, Dijon mustard, light or mayonnaise, salt, and pepper in a bowl.

2. Top each slice of whole-wheat bread with egg salad.

3. Add cucumber slices and alfalfa sprouts on top.

7. Chicken Stir-Fry with Vegetables

Total Time: 20 minutes

Nutritional Values:

· Calories: 350
· Fat: 5g
· Carbohydrates: 30g
· Fiber: 5g
· Protein: 30g
· Sugar: 5g

Ingredients:

• Four ounces of skinless, boneless chicken breast, sliced into small pieces
• Onc bell pepper, cut; • One tablespoon olive oil
• One sliced onion
• One cup of florets of broccoli
• Taste soy sauce

Guidelines:

1. The olive oil should be heated over medium-high heat in a large skillet or wok.
2. Add the chicken and cook it thoroughly.
3. Include the broccoli, onion, and bell pepper.
4. Stir-fry the veggies for five to seven minutes, or until they are soft.
5. Toss with soy sauce according to taste.

8. Turkey and Avocado Wrap with Lettuce, Tomato, and Cucumber

Total Time: 10 minutes

Nutritional Values:

· Calories: 300

· Fat: 10g

· Carbohydrates: 25g

· Fiber: 5g

· Protein: 25g

· Sugar: 2g

Ingredients:

• One large lettuce leaf; ½ avocado; 4 ounces sliced turkey;

• One tomato, chopped

• Slices of cucumber

• Tacos made of whole wheat

Guidelines:

1. Top a whole-wheat tortilla with avocado.

2. Place pieces of cucumber, tomato, lettuce, and turkey on top.

3. Tortilla rolls

9. Black Bean Soup with Whole-Wheat Tortilla Chips

Total Time: 1 hour

Nutritional Values:

· Calories: 400
· Fat: 5g
· Carbohydrates: 55g
· Fiber: 10g
· Protein: 20g
· Sugar: 5g

Ingredients:

• One cup of drained dried black beans
• A single sliced onion and two cups of veggie broth
• Whole-wheat tortilla chips; one chopped carrot. one chopped celery stalk; two minced garlic cloves; one teaspoon cumin; salt and pepper to taste

Guidelines:

1. Combine black beans, celery, carrots, onion, garlic, cumin, salt, and pepper in a big pot.
2. Bring to a boil, then lower the heat and simmer until the beans are soft about 30 minutes.
3. Puree soup using a blender or immersion blender.

4. Serve whole-wheat tortilla chips alongside the soup.

10. Grilled Chicken and Vegetable Kabobs

Total Time: 30 minutes (including grilling time)

Nutritional Values:

· Calories: 350

· Fat: 5g

· Carbohydrates: 25g

· Fiber: 5g

· Protein: 30g

· Sugar: 2g

Ingredients:

• Four ounces of cubed, skinless, boneless chicken breast

• One bell pepper, sliced into pieces

• One onion, sliced into pieces

• One zucchini, sliced into pieces

• Spray with olive oil

Guidelines:

1. Set the grill pan or grill to medium heat.

2. Thread bell pepper, onion, zucchini, and chicken onto skewers.

3. Mist skewers with a spray of olive oil.

4. Cook the skewers for ten to fifteen minutes, or until the vegetables are soft and the chicken is thoroughly cooked.

11. Quinoa Salad with Roasted Vegetables and Feta Cheese

Total Time: 45 minutes

Nutritional Values:

· Calories: 400

· Fat: 10g

· Carbohydrates: 40g

· Fiber: 5g

· Protein: 15g

· Sugar: 5g

Ingredients:

• Two cups vegetable broth; one diced red bell pepper; one cup washed quinoa

• 1/4 cup crumbled feta cheese

• 1 sliced zucchini

• 1 chopped onion

• Olive oil spray

• Add pepper and salt to taste.

Guidelines:
1. Set oven temperature to 400 F or 200 C.
2. Combine salt, pepper, and olive oil spritz with bell pepper, zucchini, and onion.
3. After spreading the vegetables out on a baking sheet, roast them for 20 to 25 minutes, or until they are soft.
4. Prepare the quinoa per the instructions on the package while the veggies roast.
5. Combine the cooked quinoa, feta cheese, and roasted veggies in a big bowl.
6. Toss to cover.

12. Lentil and Vegetable Stew

Total Time: 1 hour

Nutritional Values:

· Calories: 350
· Fat: 5g
· Carbohydrates: 50g
· Fiber: 10g
· Protein: 15g
· Sugar: 5g

Ingredients:

• One cup of washed dried lentils
• A single sliced onion and two cups of veggie broth
• One sliced carrot; one chopped celery stalk; two minced garlic cloves; one teaspoon dried thyme
• Add pepper and salt to taste.

Guidelines:

Lentils, vegetable broth, onion, carrot, celery, garlic, thyme, salt, and pepper should all be combined in a big saucepan.

2. Bring to a boil, then lower the heat and simmer until the lentils are soft about 30 minutes.

3. In the final ten minutes of simmering, add any extra veggies, like chopped spinach or diced tomatoes.

4. Present stew warm.

13. Turkey and Avocado Salad with Whole-Wheat Crackers

Total Time: 15 minutes

Nutritional Values:

· Calories: 300

· Fat: 10g

· Carbohydrates: 25g

· Fiber: 5g

· Protein: 20g

· Sugar: 2g

Ingredients:

• ½ sliced avocado; • 4 ounces sliced turkey; • 1 tablespoon lemon juice

• Add pepper and salt to taste.

• Whole-grain crackers

Guidelines:

1. Put the turkey, avocado, lemon juice, salt, and pepper in a bowl.

2. Toss in the coat.

3. Use whole-wheat crackers to serve the salad.

14. Leftover Roasted Chicken Salad with Grapes and Walnuts

Total Time: 10 minutes

Nutritional Values:

· Calories: 350
· Fat: 10g
· Carbohydrates: 30g
· Fiber: 5g
· Protein: 30g
· Sugar: 5g

Ingredients:

• 1/4 cup halved grapes • 1/4 cup chopped walnuts
• 4 ounces minced cooked chicken
• Two teaspoons of light or mayonnaise
• Add pepper and salt to taste.

Guidelines:

1. Put the cooked chicken, walnuts, grapes, light or mayonnaise, salt, and pepper in a bowl.
2. Toss in the coat.

15. Tuna Salad Stuffed Tomatoes

Total Time: 15 minutes

Nutritional Values:
- Calories: 300
- Fat: 10g
- Carbohydrates: 20g
- Fiber: 5g
- Protein: 20g
- Sugar: 2g

Ingredients:
- Three ounces of drained canned tuna
- ¼ cup chopped celery
- two tablespoons mayonnaise, either light or regular
- 2 large tomatoes, cut in half; • 1 tablespoon minced onion; • Salt and pepper to taste

Guidelines:
1. Place the tuna, celery, onion, light or mayonnaise, salt, and pepper in a bowl.
2. Remove the tomato halves' seeds and pulp with a spoon.
3. Stuff tuna salad into tomato halves.

16. Cottage Cheese with Fruit and Nuts

Total Time: 5 minutes

Nutritional Values:

· Calories: 300
· Fat: 5g
· Carbohydrates: 30g
· Fiber: 5g
· Protein: 20g
· Sugar: 10g

Ingredients:

A cup of cottage cheese, ½ cup of mixed berries, and ¼ cup of chopped nuts (pecans, walnuts, and almonds)

Guidelines:

1. Fill a glass or bowl with cottage cheese, chopped almonds, and mixed berries.

17. Whole-wheat toast with Avocado and Egg

Total Time: 5 minutes

Nutritional Values:

· Calories: 300

· Fat: 10g

· Carbohydrates: 35g

· Fiber: 5g

· Protein: 15g

· Sugar: 2g

Ingredients:

• One egg; two slices of whole-wheat bread; one mashed avocado;

Guidelines:

1. Spread each slice of whole-wheat bread with mashed avocado.

2. Place a fried or poached egg on top.

18. Black Bean and Avocado Quesadillas

Total Time: 15 minutes

Nutritional Values:

· Calories: 350

· Fat: 15g

· Carbohydrates: 30g

· Fiber: 5g

· Protein: 20g

· Sugar: 2g

Ingredients:

• One whole-wheat tortilla; ¼ cup black bean puree; ¼ cup avocado puree

• Cheese that has been shredded

Guidelines:

1. On half of a whole-wheat tortilla, spread mashed avocado and black beans.

2. Add some cheese shredded on top.

3. In a skillet over medium heat, fold the tortilla in half and cook until the cheese melts and the tortilla turns golden brown.

Dinner Recipes

1. Baked Salmon with Roasted Vegetables
Total Time: 30 minutes (including baking time)
Nutritional Values:
· Calories: 400
· Fat: 15g
· Carbohydrates: 25g
· Fiber: 5g
· Protein: 35g
· Sugar: 5g

Ingredients:
• One sliced bell pepper
• Four ounces of fish fillet
• One sliced onion
• One sliced zucchini
 • Olive oil spray
• Toppings of salt and pepper

Guidelines:
1. Set the oven's temperature to 400 degrees Fahrenheit, or 200 degrees Celsius.
2. Combine salt, pepper, and olive oil spray on veggies.
3. After spreading the vegetables out on a baking sheet, roast them for 20 to 25 minutes, or until they are soft.
4. Arrange the salmon fillet on a different parchment paper-lined baking sheet while the vegetables roast.
5. Season fish with salt and pepper and drizzle with olive oil.
6. Bake the salmon for 12 to 15 minutes, or until it is well done.
7. Accompany fish with roasted veggies.

2. Chicken Stir-Fry with Broccoli and Brown Rice

Total Time: 20 minutes

Nutritional Values:

· Calories: 400
· Fat: 10g
· Carbohydrates: 40g
· Fiber: 5g
· Protein: 30g
· Sugar: 5g

Ingredients:

• Four ounces of skinless, boneless chicken breast, sliced into small pieces
• 1 head of broccoli with florets; • 1 tablespoon olive oil
• One cup of brown rice, cooked
• Taste soy sauce

Guidelines:

1. The olive oil should be heated over medium-high heat in a large skillet or wok.
2. Add the chicken and cook it thoroughly.
3. Stir-fry the broccoli for 5 to 7 minutes, or until it becomes soft.
4. Stir-fry the cooked brown rice until it is well hot.
5. Toss with soy sauce according to taste.

3. Marinara sauce and whole-wheat pasta paired with turkey meatballs

Total Time: 1 hour (including baking time)

Nutritional Values:

· Calories: 450

· Fat: 15g

· Carbohydrates: 55g

· Fiber: 5g

· Protein: 30g

· Sugar: 10g

Ingredients:

• 1/2 cup minced onion; 1 pound ground turkey; and 1/2 cup crumbled bread crumbs

• Whole-wheat pasta • Marinara sauce • One egg • Salt and pepper to taste

Guidelines:

1. Set oven temperature to 400 F or 200 C.

2. Combine the ground turkey, bread crumbs, onion, egg, salt, and pepper in a big basin.

3. Shape dough into meatballs.

4. Transfer meatballs to a parchment paper-lined baking sheet.

5. Bake meatballs for twenty to twenty-five minutes, or until done.

6. Prepare whole-wheat pasta as directed on the packet.

7. Transfer the drained pasta to a big bowl.

8. Combine meatballs and marinara sauce with pasta.

4. Baked Cod with Roasted Asparagus and Lemon

Total Time: 30 minutes (including baking time)
Nutritional Values:
· Calories: 350
· Fat: 10g
· Carbohydrates: 20g
· Fiber: 5g
· Protein: 30g
· Sugar: 3g

Ingredients:
• One bunch of trimmed asparagus; four ounces of cod fillet; and olive oil spray
• Add pepper and salt to taste.
• One sliced lemon

Guidelines:
1. Set the oven's temperature to 400 degrees Fahrenheit, or 200 degrees Celsius.
2. Combine salt, pepper, and olive oil spritz with asparagus.
3. Arrange the asparagus on a baking tray and cook it for 15 to 20 minutes, or until it becomes soft.
4. Put the fish fillet on a different baking sheet covered with parchment paper and roast the asparagus at the same time.

5. Season cod with salt and pepper and drizzle with olive oil.

6. Bake the fish for ten to twelve minutes, or until it's done.

7. Place lemon slices and roasted asparagus on top of the cod.

5. Veggie Burger on Whole-Wheat Bun with Lettuce, Tomato, and Onion

Total Time: 30 minutes

Nutritional Values:

· Calories: 350
· Fat: 5g
· Carbohydrates: 40g
· Fiber: 5g
· Protein: 30g
· Sugar: 5g

Ingredients:

One whole-wheat baguette, one vegetarian burger, and lettuce leaves

• Slicing tomatoes • Slicing onions

Guidelines:

1. Prepare the veggie burger according to the guidelines on the package.

2. Spread whole-wheat bread.

3. Place lettuce, tomato, onion, and veggie burger on top of bun.

6. Turkey and Avocado Wrap with Lettuce, Tomato, and Cucumber

Total Time: 10 minutes
Nutritional Values:
· Calories: 300
· Fat: 10g
· Carbohydrates: 25g
· Fiber: 5g
· Protein: 25g
· Sugar: 2g

Ingredients:
• One large lettuce leaf; ½ avocado; 4 ounces sliced turkey;
• One tomato, chopped
• Slices of cucumber
• Tacos made of whole wheat

Guidelines:
1. Top a whole-wheat tortilla with avocado.
2. Place pieces of cucumber, tomato, lettuce, and turkey on top.
3. Wrap the tortilla and savor it!

7. Grilled Shrimp with Roasted Vegetables and Quinoa

Total Time: 30 minutes (including grilling time)
Nutritional Values:
· Calories: 400
· Fat: 10g
· Carbohydrates: 35g
· Fiber: 5g
· Protein: 35g
· Sugar: 5g

Ingredients:
• One pound of peeled and deveined shrimp; one chopped bell pepper; one chopped onion
• Cooked quinoa; • Olive oil spray; • Chopped zucchini; • Salt and pepper to taste

Guidelines:
1. Turn the heat up to medium-high on the grill or grill pan.
2. Attach prawns to skewers.
3. Add salt and pepper to the skewers after misting them with olive oil spray.
4. Cook shrimp on the grill for 5 to 7 minutes on each side, or until done.
5. Put the cooked quinoa, bell pepper, onion, and zucchini in a big bowl.
6. Add salt, pepper, and olive oil spray.
7. Present the grilled shrimp among vegetables and quinoa.

8. Turkey and Vegetable Stir-Fry

Total Time: 20 minutes

Nutritional Values:

· Calories: 350

· Fat: 5g

· Carbohydrates: 30g

· Fiber: 5g

· Protein: 30g

· Sugar: 5g

Ingredients:

• Four ounces of skinless, boneless turkey breast, sliced into small pieces

• One bell pepper, cut; • One tablespoon olive oil

• One sliced onion

• One cup of florets of broccoli

• Taste soy sauce

Guidelines:

1. The olive oil should be heated over medium-high heat in a large skillet or wok.

2. Add the turkey and boil it thoroughly.

3. Include the broccoli, onion, and bell pepper.

4. Stir-fry the veggies for five to seven minutes, or until they are soft.

5. Toss with soy sauce according to taste.

9. Grilled Chicken Fajitas with Whole-Wheat Tortillas

Total Time: 30 minutes (including grilling time)
Nutritional Values:
· Calories: 400
· Fat: 10g
· Carbohydrates: 40g
· Fiber: 5g
· Protein: 35g
· Sugar: 5g

Ingredients:
• Four ounces of sliced, skinless, boneless chicken breast
• Slabbed one bell pepper
• One sliced onion
• Whole-wheat tortillas; • Olive oil spray
 • Salted and pepper to taste
 • Your preferred toppings (shredded cheese, salsa, and sour cream)

Guidelines:

1. Turn the heat up to medium-high on the grill or grill pan.

2. Thread vegetables and chicken onto skewers.

3. Add salt and pepper to the skewers after misting them with olive oil spray.

4. Grill the skewers for five to seven minutes on each side or until the veggies are soft and the chicken is cooked through.

5. Use an oven or skillet to reheat tortillas.

6. Stuff veggies and grilled chicken into tortillas.

7. Add your preferred toppings on top.

10. Baked Tofu with Roasted Vegetables

Total Time: 30 minutes (including baking time)

Nutritional Values:

· Calories: 350

· Fat: 10g

· Carbohydrates: 30g

· Fiber: 5g

· Protein: 25g

· Sugar: 5g

Ingredients:

• One extra-firm block of tofu, dried off and sliced into cubes

• One sliced bell pepper

• One chopped onion

• One sliced zucchini; • Olive oil spray; • Toppings of salt and pepper

Guidelines:

1. Set oven temperature to 400 F or 200 C.

2. Combine salt, pepper, and olive oil spritz with the tofu.

3. Transfer the tofu onto a parchment paper-lined baking sheet.

4. Combine salt, pepper, and olive oil spray on veggies.

5. Arrange veggies all around the tofu.

6. Bake for 20 to 25 minutes or until the vegetables are soft and the tofu is golden brown.

11. Grilled Flank Steak with Roasted Asparagus and Quinoa

Total Time: 30 minutes (including grilling time)

Nutritional Values:

· Calories: 400
· Fat: 15g
· Carbohydrates: 30g
· Fiber: 5g
· Protein: 35g
· Sugar: 5g

Ingredients:

• One pound of flank steak; one bunch of trimmed asparagus; and olive oil spray
• Add pepper and salt to taste.
• Prepared quinoa

Guidelines:

1. Turn the heat up to medium-high on the grill or grill pan.
2. Apply olive oil spray to flank steak and sprinkle with salt & pepper.
3. Cook the steak on the grill for 5 to 7 minutes on each side, or until the doneness you choose.
4. Toss asparagus with salt, pepper, and olive oil spray while the steak is grilling.
5. Roast asparagus on a baking sheet for ten to fifteen minutes, or until it is soft.
6. Present the steak with quinoa and roasted asparagus.

12. Chicken and Vegetable Skewers with Teriyaki Sauce

Total Time: 30 minutes (including grilling time)

Nutritional Values:

· Calories: 350
· Fat: 10g
· Carbohydrates: 30g
· Fiber: 5g
· Protein: 30g
· Sugar: 5g

Ingredients:

• Four ounces of skinless, boneless chicken breast, sliced into small pieces
• One bell pepper, sliced into pieces
• One onion, sliced into pieces
• One zucchini, sliced into pieces
• Sauce Teriyaki
• Spray with olive oil

Guidelines:

1. Turn the heat up to medium-high on the grill or grill pan.
2. Thread vegetables and chicken onto skewers.
3. Apply teriyaki sauce and olive oil spray on the skewers.
4. Grill the skewers for five to seven minutes on each side or until the veggies are soft and the chicken is cooked through.
5. Garnish the skewers with extra teriyaki sauce.

Snack recipes

1. Greek Yogurt with Berries and Granola
Total Time: 5 minutes
Nutritional Values:
· Calories: 300
· Fat: 5g
· Carbohydrates: 40g
· Fiber: 5g
· Protein: 20g
· Sugar: 15g
Ingredients:
• One cup of Greek yogurt, plain
• ½ cup of granola; ¼ cup of mixed berries
Guidelines:
1. Fill a glass or bowl with yogurt, mixed berries, and granola.

2. Cottage Cheese with Pineapple and Nuts

Total Time: 5 minutes
Nutritional Values:
· Calories: 300
· Fat: 5g
· Carbohydrates: 35g
· Fiber: 5g
· Protein: 20g
· Sugar: 10g

Ingredients:

• ½ cup sliced pineapple
 One-fourth cup finely chopped nuts (pecans, walnuts, and almonds)
1 cup cottage cheese

Guidelines:

1. In a glass or bowl, layer cottage cheese, chopped almonds, and diced pineapple.

3. Celery Sticks with Peanut Butter

Total Time: 2 minutes

Nutritional Values:

· Calories: 200
· Fat: 10g
· Carbohydrates: 7g
· Fiber: 2g
· Protein: 7g
· Sugar: 3g

Ingredients:

• Peanut butter • Celery sticks

Guidelines

1. Drizzle celery sticks with peanut butter.

4. Apple Slices with Almond Butter

Total Time: 2 minutes

Nutritional Values:

· Calories: 180
· Fat: 8g
· Carbohydrates: 25g
· Fiber: 4g
· Protein: 3g
· Sugar: 20g

Ingredients:

• Almond butter • Apple slices

Guidelines:

1. Drizzle apple slices with almond butter.

5. Trail Mix

Total Time: 5 minutes

Nutritional Values:

· Calories: 200

· Fat: 10g

· Carbohydrates: 20g

· Fiber: 3g

· Protein: 4g

· Sugar: 10g

Ingredients:

• Nuts (pecans, walnuts, and almonds)

• Seeds (chia, pumpkin, and sunflower seeds)

• Canned fruit, including raisins, cranberries, and apricots

Guidelines:

1. In a bowl, mix together nuts, seeds, and dried fruit.

6. Rice Cakes with Avocado

Total Time: 3 minutes

Nutritional Values:

· Calories: 180

· Fat: 10g

· Carbohydrates: 25g

· Fiber: 3g

· Protein: 4g

· Sugar: 1g

Ingredients:

• Cakes made of rice

• Slicked avocado

Guidelines:

1. Place avocado slices on top of rice cakes.

7. Air-Popped Popcorn

Total Time: 3 minutes

Nutritional Values:

· Calories: 110
· Fat: 1g
· Carbohydrates: 25g
· Fiber: 3g
· Protein: 3g
· Sugar: 1g

Ingredients:

• Kernels of popcorn

Guidelines:

1. Fill an air popper with popcorn kernels.
2. Pop popcorn as directed by the maker.

8. Cucumber Slices with Cream Cheese

Total Time: 2 minutes

Nutritional Values:

· Calories: 150
· Fat: 5g
· Carbohydrates: 10g
· Fiber: 1g
· Protein: 3g
· Sugar: 1g

Ingredients:

• Slices of cucumber; • Cream cheese

Guidelines:

1. Spread cucumber slices with cream cheese.

9. Roasted Edamame

Total Time: 15 minutes

Nutritional Values:

· Calories: 180

· Fat: 7g

· Carbohydrates: 15g

· Fiber: 4g

· Protein: 11g

· Sugar: 2g

Ingredients:

• Olive oil mist; To-taste salt and pepper

• Frozen edamame

Guidelines:

1. Set oven temperature to 400 F or 200 C.

2. Add salt, pepper, and olive oil spray to the edamame.

3. Arrange the edamame evenly on a parchment paper-lined baking sheet.

4. Roast until soft, 10 to 15 minutes.

10. Greek Yogurt Parfait with Berries and Chia Seeds

Total Time: 5 minutes

Nutritional Values:

· Calories: 350

· Fat: 5g

· Carbohydrates: 45g

· Fiber: 5g

· Protein: 20g

· Sugar: 15g

Ingredients:

• One cup of Greek yogurt, plain

• 1/4 cup of mixed berries; • 1/4 cup of chia seeds

Guidelines:

1. In a glass or bowl, arrange yogurt, mixed berries, and chia seeds.

2. Chia seeds should be chilled for at least half an hour, or until they have soaked and thickened.

11. Turkey and Avocado Roll-Ups

Total Time: 5 minutes

Nutritional Values:

· Calories: 200

· Fat: 10g

· Carbohydrates: 5g

· Fiber: 2g

· Protein: 15g

· Sugar: 1g

Ingredients:

• Avocado slices; Whole-wheat tortillas
 Turkey slices

Guidelines:

1. Arrange slices of avocado on tortillas.

2. Add slices of turkey on top.

3. Fold tortillas in half.

12. Cottage Cheese with Cucumber and Herbs

Total Time: 5 minutes

Nutritional Values:

· Calories: 200

· Fat: 5g

· Carbohydrates: 10g

· Fiber: 1g

· Protein: 18g

· Sugar: 2g

Ingredients:

• One cup cottage cheese; ½ cup diced cucumber; chopped fresh herbs (parsley, dill, and chives);

Guidelines:

1. In a glass or bowl, layer cottage cheese, diced cucumber, and chopped herbs.

13. Roasted Sweet Potato Sticks

Total Time: 15 minutes

Nutritional Values:

· Calories: 200

· Fat: 4g

· Carbohydrates: 35g

· Fiber: 4g

· Protein: 2g

· Sugar: 15g

Ingredients:

• Peel and cut into sticks the sweet potato

• Mist with olive oil

• Adjust with salt and pepper.

Guidelines:

1. Set oven temperature to 400 F or 200 C.

2. Combine salt, pepper, and olive oil spray with the sweet potato sticks.

3. Arrange the sweet potato sticks on a parchment paper-lined baking sheet.

4. Roast for 15 to 20 minutes, or until crispy but still soft.

14. Chocolate Avocado Smoothie

Total Time: 5 minutes

Nutritional Values:

· Calories: 300
· Fat: 15g
· Carbohydrates: 30g
· Fiber: 5g
· Protein: 5g
· Sugar: 10g

Ingredients:

• 1/2 avocado and 1 cup almond milk without sugar
• One scoop of powdered chocolate protein.
• One tablespoon of powdered cocoa
• One teaspoon of honey, if desired

Guidelines:

1. Put all the ingredients in a blender and process until they are smooth.

15. Apple Slices with Cinnamon and Honey

Total Time: 5 minutes

Nutritional Values:

· Calories: 150
· Fat: 0g
· Carbohydrates: 38g
· Fiber: 4g
· Protein: 1g
· Sugar: 20g

Ingredients:

• Honey (optional) • Cinnamon • Apple slices

Guidelines:

1. Drizzle slices of apple with cinnamon.
2. If desired, drizzle with honey.

16. Rice Cakes with Peanut Butter and Banana

Total Time: 3 minutes

Nutritional Values:

· Calories: 250
· Fat: 10g
· Carbohydrates: 35g
· Fiber: 4g
· Protein: 5g
· Sugar: 10g

Ingredients:

• Peanut butter; rice cakes; banana slices

Guidelines:

Spread rice cakes with peanut butter.

2. Add slices of banana on top.

Dessert recipes

1. Baked Apples with Cinnamon and Honey

Total Time: 30 minutes (including baking time)

Nutritional Values:

· Calories: 200

· Fat: 2g

· Carbohydrates: 40g

· Fiber: 5g

· Protein: 1g

· Sugar: 15g

Ingredients:

• Two cored and sliced apples;

• One teaspoon cinnamon

• One tablespoon honey

Guidelines:

Set the oven temperature to 175 degrees Celsius, or 350 degrees Fahrenheit.

2. Line a baking dish with apple slices.

3. Add a honey and cinnamon sprinkle.

4. Bake the apples for 20 to 25 minutes, or until they are soft.

2. Chia Seed Pudding with Berries

Total Time: 5 minutes (plus soaking time)

Nutritional Values:

· Calories: 300

· Fat: 10g

· Carbohydrates: 35g

· Fiber: 10g

· Protein: 10g

· Sugar: 10g

Ingredients:

• 1/4 cup almond milk without sugar; ½ cup chia seeds; and ¼ cup mixed fruit

• One tablespoon of honey, if desired

Guidelines:

1. Put almond milk and chia seeds in a basin or jar.

2. Give it a good stir, cover, and chill for at least two hours or overnight.

3. If preferred, sprinkle honey and mixed berries on top.

3. Baked Pears with Ginger and Maple Syrup

Total Time: 30 minutes (including baking time)

Nutritional Values:

· Calories: 250

· Fat: 2g

· Carbohydrates: 50g

· Fiber: 6g

· Protein: 2g

· Sugar: 20g

Ingredients:

• One teaspoon ground ginger;

• two pears, cored and cut in half

• One tablespoon of maple syrup

Guidelines:

Set the oven temperature to 175 degrees Celsius, or 350 degrees Fahrenheit.

2. Put the pear halves in a dish for baking.

3. Drizzle with maple syrup and sprinkle with ginger.

4. Bake the pears for 20 to 25 minutes, or until they are soft.

4. No-Bake Chocolate Avocado Mousse

Total Time: 15 minutes

Nutritional Values:

· Calories: 350
· Fat: 25g
· Carbohydrates: 30g
· Fiber: 5g
· Protein: 10g
· Sugar: 15g

Ingredients:

One peeled and mashed avocado and one-third cup of unsweetened cocoa powder

• Two tsp honey

• One tsp vanilla extract; one pinch of salt;

Guidelines:

1. Put the mashed avocado, cocoa powder, honey, vanilla essence, and salt in a food processor.
2. Blend until creamy and smooth.
3. Distribute mousse into bowls or glasses.
4. Chill for a minimum of half an hour or until solidified.

5. Baked Cinnamon Apples with Greek Yogurt

Total Time: 30 minutes (including baking time)

Nutritional Values:

· Calories: 250
· Fat: 5g
· Carbohydrates: 45g
· Fiber: 5g
· Protein: 15g
· Sugar: 15g

Ingredients:

• Two cored and sliced apples
 • One teaspoon cinnamon
 • One tablespoon honey
• One cup of Greek yogurt, plain

Guidelines:

Set the oven temperature to 175 degrees Celsius, or 350 degrees Fahrenheit.

2. Line a baking dish with apple slices.

3. Add a honey and cinnamon sprinkle.

4. Bake the apples for 20 to 25 minutes, or until they are soft.

5. Add Greek yogurt on top.

6. Dark Chocolate-Dipped Strawberries

Total Time: 15 minutes (plus chilling time)
Nutritional Values:
· Calories: 150 (per serving)
· Fat: 8g
· Carbohydrates: 15g
· Fiber: 2g
· Protein: 2g
· Sugar: 10g

Ingredients:
• 12 hulled strawberries
• Four ounces of melted dark chocolate

Guidelines:
1. Make sure to line a baking sheet with parchment paper.
2. Soak each strawberry in chocolate that has melted.
3. After placing it on parchment paper, chill the chocolate until it solidifies.

7. No-Bake Mango Cheesecake

Total Time: 30 minutes (plus chilling time)
Nutritional Values:

· Calories: 250 (per slice)
· Fat: 12g
· Carbohydrates: 25g
· Fiber: 3g
· Protein: 6g
· Sugar: 15g

Ingredients:

• ¼ cup melted butter; 1 cup plain Greek yogurt; and 1 cup graham cracker crumbs
• 1/4 cup honey; ½ cup mashed mango; ½ teaspoon vanilla essence

Guidelines:

1. Grains from graham crackers and melted butter should be combined in a bowl.
2. Press into the bottom of a spring form pan or pie dish.
3. Combine Greek yogurt, mashed mango, honey, and vanilla extract in another bowl.
4. Transfer the filling to the crust.
5. Chill for a minimum of two hours or until solidified.

8. Baked Cinnamon-Sugar Plums

Total Time: 25 minutes (including baking time)

Nutritional Values:

· Calories: 200

· Fat: 1g

· Carbohydrates: 45g

· Fiber: 3g

· Protein: 1g

· Sugar: 15g

Ingredients:

• One tablespoon of ground cinnamon

• two teaspoons of honey; twelve halved plums

Guidelines:

Set the oven temperature to 175 degrees Celsius, or 350 degrees Fahrenheit

2. Put the halves of the plum in a baking dish.

3. After adding a cinnamon sprinkle, drizzle with honey.

4. Bake until plums are soft, 15 to 20 minutes.

9. No-Bake Chocolate Peanut Butter Cups

Total Time: 20 minutes (plus freezing time)

Nutritional Values:

· Calories: 200 (per cup)
· Fat: 12g
· Carbohydrates: 10g
· Fiber: 2g
· Protein: 5g
· Sugar: 10g

Ingredients:

• One-half cup peanut butter
• ¼ cup cocoa powder, unsweetened
• Two tsp honey
• Tiny cupcake cases.

Guidelines:

1. Place cupcake liners inside a small muffin tray.
2. Mix honey, cocoa powder, and peanut butter in a bowl.
3. Stir until thoroughly mixed.
4. Spoon mixture into cupcake liners in heaping spoonfuls.
5. Chill for a minimum of half an hour or until solidified.

10. No-Bake Oatmeal Raisin Cookies

Total Time: 15 minutes (plus chilling time)
Nutritional Values:
· Calories: 150 (per cookie)
· Fat: 5g
· Carbohydrates: 25g
· Fiber: 3g
· Protein: 3g
· Sugar: 10g

Ingredients:

• ¼ cup raisins • ¼ cup peanut butter • 1 cup rolled oats

• Two tsp honey

Guidelines:

1. Put the rolled oats, honey, peanut butter, and raisins in a bowl.

2. Stir until thoroughly mixed.

3. Spoon the mixture onto a baking sheet lined with paper.

4. Chill for a minimum of half an hour or until solidified.

11. No-Bake Almond Joy Bites

Total Time: 15 minutes (plus freezing time)
Nutritional Values:

· Calories: 100 (per bite)
· Fat: 7g
· Carbohydrates: 8g
· Fiber: 1g
· Protein: 2g
· Sugar: 6g

Ingredients:

• One-half cup almond butter
• ¼ cup cocoa powder, unsweetened
• Two tsp honey
• A tsp of coconut extract
• Optional coconut shreds

Guidelines:

1. Put almond butter, coconut extract, honey, and cocoa powder in a bowl.
2. Stir until thoroughly mixed.
3. Shape the mixture into spheres.
4. If preferred, roll the balls with coconut shreds.
5. Freeze until solid, which should take at least 30 minutes.

12. No-Bake Banana Bread Bites

Total Time: 20 minutes (plus chilling time)

Nutritional Values:

· Calories: 150 (per bite)

· Fat: 4g

· Carbohydrates: 25g

· Fiber: 3g

· Protein: 2g

· Sugar: 13g

Ingredients:

• Mashed 1 ripe banana

• 1/4 cup almond butter; 1/4 cup rolled oats

• Two tsp honey

• One-half teaspoon of cinnamon

Guidelines:

1. Put the mashed banana, rolled oats, honey, cinnamon, and almond butter in a bowl.

2. Stir until thoroughly mixed.

3. Shape the mixture into spheres.

4. Chill for a minimum of half an hour or until solid.

13. No-Bake Fruit and Yogurt Parfaits

Total Time: 10 minutes

Nutritional Values:

· Calories: 300 (per parfait)

· Fat: 5g

· Carbohydrates: 45g

· Fiber: 5g

· Protein: 10g

· Sugar: 15g

Ingredients:

• One cup of Greek yogurt, plain

• ½ cup of granola; ¼ cup of mixed berries

Guidelines:

1. Fill a glass or bowl with yogurt, mixed berries, and granola.

14. No-Bake Chocolate Avocado Truffles

Total Time: 15 minutes (plus chilling time)

Nutritional Values:

· Calories: 150 (per truffle)

· Fat: 10g

· Carbohydrates: 10g

· Fiber: 2g

· Protein: 3g

· Sugar: 7g

Ingredients:

• Half an avocado, pitted and blended; • One-third cup unsweetened cocoa powder

• Two tsp honey

• One tsp vanilla extract

• Dusting cocoa powder (optional)

Guidelines:

1. Put the mashed avocado, honey, cocoa powder, and vanilla extract in a bowl.

2. Stir until thoroughly mixed.

3. Shape the mixture into spheres.

4. If preferred, sprinkle some chocolate powder over the balls.

5. Chill for a minimum of half an hour, or until solid.

15. No-Bake Pumpkin Pie Parfaits

Total Time: 10 minutes

Nutritional Values:

· Calories: 350 (per parfait)
· Fat: 10g
· Carbohydrates: 50g
· Fiber: 5g
· Protein: 10g
· Sugar: 20g

Ingredients:

• ¼ cup plain Greek yogurt; 1 cup canned pumpkin puree
• Two tsp honey
• 1/2 tsp ground ginger; 1/2 tsp nutmeg; 1/2 tsp cinnamon; and 1/4 cup granola

Guidelines:

1. Combine the pumpkin puree, Greek yogurt, honey, nutmeg, cinnamon, and ginger in a bowl.
2. Stir until thoroughly mixed.
3. In a glass or bowl, arrange the yogurt mixture and granola.

16. No-Bake Coffee and Chocolate Energy Bites

Total Time: 15 minutes (plus chilling time)

Nutritional Values:

· Calories: 150 (per bite)

· Fat: 5g

· Carbohydrates: 15g

· Fiber: 3g

· Protein: 3g

· Sugar: 5g

Ingredients:

• A quarter of a cup of strong coffee

• ¼ cup cocoa powder, unsweetened

• One-third cup of rolled oats

• One tablespoon of almond, peanut, or cashew butter; two tablespoons of honey

Guidelines:

1. Put the rolled oats, honey, nut butter, cocoa powder, and boiled coffee in a bowl.

2. Stir until thoroughly mixed.

3. Shape the mixture into spheres.

4. Chill for a minimum of half an hour or until solid.

Conclusion

Adopting a Diabetic Lifestyle That Is Friendly to Your Gallbladder

For those who need help striking a delicate balance between gallbladder health and diabetes management, the Gallbladder Diet Cookbook for Diabetes is a great resource. In addition to offering a wide variety of delectable recipes, this cookbook highlights the significance of mindful eating catered to the particular requirements of individuals dealing with chronic health issues.

People with diabetes can adopt a diabetes-friendly diet and actively support gallbladder health by preparing the delicious recipes found in this cookbook. The well-balanced meals highlight entire, high-nutrient foods that help maintain stable blood sugar levels and improve the health of the gallbladder in general.

The cookbook also promotes a holistic approach to health, taking into account variables other than dietary decisions. It highlights the need to maintain a healthy weight, drink plenty of water, and get regular exercise—all crucial elements of an all-encompassing plan for controlling diabetes and promoting gallbladder function.

People are not only embarking on a delicious trip but also making well-informed decisions that support their health objectives as they peruse the enticing recipes in this cookbook. At the end of the day, the Gallbladder Diet Cookbook for Diabetes encourages people to enjoy tasty, health-conscious meals and to build a positive association between.

MEAL PLANNER

WEEK 1 MEAL PLANNER

	BREAKFAST	LUNCH	DINNER	SNACKS	DESSERT
MON					
TUE					
WED					
THU					
FRI					
SUN					

Gallbladder Diet Cookbook for Diabetes

WEEK 2 MEAL PLANNER

	BREAKFAST	LUNCH	DINNER	SNACKS	DESSERT
MON					
TUE					
WED					
THU					
FRI					
SAT					
SUN					

Gallbladder Diet Cookbook for Diabetes

WEEK 3 MEAL PLANNER

	BREAKFAST	LUNCH	DINNER	SNACKS	DESSERT
MON					
TUE					
WED					
THU					
FRI					
SAT					
SUN					

Gallbladder Diet Cookbook for Diabetes

WEEK 4 MEAL PLANNER

	BREAKFAST	LUNCH	DINNER	SNACKS	DESSERT
MON					
TUE					
WED					
THU					
FRI					
SAT					
SUN					

Gallbladder Diet Cookbook for Diabetes

Printed in Great Britain
by Amazon

39471053R00086